130 THINGS
YOU SHOULD KNOW ABOUT
ED SHEERAN

By Gordon Law

Printed in Europe and the USA
ISBN-13: 978-1979189453
ISBN-10: 1979189455

ED SHEERAN

HIS RISE FROM SOFA-SURFER TO MUSIC SUPERSTAR

By Gordon Law

Also available to buy

Introduction

Ed Sheeran has become a megastar in music, selling millions of records and performing at packed-out stadiums all over the world.

With his trusty guitar in hand, Ed is able to excite thousands of screaming fans with his heart-felt ballads and catchy tunes.

He has platinum-selling albums and been recognised by the industry with many awards, including two Grammys and four BRITs.

From humble beginnings in Suffolk, right up to his headline-closing show at Glastonbury, this book gives you the low-down on the pop star's amazing career in fun, bite-sized facts.

Did you know, for example, that Ed has been given the title Baron von Edward Sheeran of

Sealand, which is an independent state located off the sea of East Anglia?

And that Ed has a custom-built pub in his garden – linked to his house by a tunnel – along with a mini zoo where he keeps animals such as barn owls, hedgehogs and otters?

Or even his song Shape of You is the seventh most-watched YouTube music video of all time with more than two billion views?

You can find out how Bruno Mars helped Ed get signed by Atlantic Records, and all the TV shows he has had cameo appearances in.

Packed with trivia, stats and information, this resource gives you the essential know-how on everything Ed Sheeran.

Ed Sheeran

Ed met Jamie Foxx after the manager of the movie star was impressed by one of his gigs in Los Angeles. Jamie invited Ed on to his radio show and even let him stay at his house where he used his studio for free. Ed had planned to get a writing session with James Bourne from Busted but lined up so many urban LA gigs that he ran out of time.

****

Gordon Burns, presenter of popular TV game show *The Krypton Factor* for 18 years, is Ed's second cousin.

Ed has given his award-winning record plaques to friends as party gifts. "You come round my flat and you come away with a plaque," he said. "There are only so many you can put on the wall without looking like a douchebag. So I prefer for my friends to celebrate the success as well and have it in their living room."

****

Ed's dad John is an art curator and lecturer, while mum Imogen has worked for the National Portrait Gallery and Manchester City Galleries.

The video for Ed's breakout song *The A Team* features actress friend Selina MacDonald and was put together by her photographer pal. Selina played Angel from the song and the entire video cost £20 – the price of a crack pipe and some fishnet tights.

****

In 2015, Ed made an appearance on a live episode of US sitcom *Undateable*. The singer performs *Thinking Out Loud* at an open-mic night, before being led off the stage by the host, who doesn't recognise who he is.

Ed Sheeran

When he was first starting out, music executives told Ed to stop using a loop pedal and rapping in his gigs. They also didn't like one of his most popular live songs *You Need Me, I Don't Need You* and claimed *Lego House* would not be a hit. Fortunately, Ed ignored their advice.

****

One of Ed's cousins, Jethro Sheeran, is a rapper who goes by the stage name Alonestar and has worked with him on some tracks.

Ed Sheeran

Ed performed at the Beatles' 50th anniversary TV special in the US in 2014. After the show, Ed had a margarita with Paul McCartney who signed a rare 1960s Hofner bass guitar for the Suffolk singer.

****

Music producer Jake Gosling was the first one Ed hit it off with and they have worked together since his *You Need Me* EP. Ed lived at his house in Surrey for a while and ended up becoming godfather to one of his children.

When he was 14, Ed got into folk/hip-hop duo Nizlopi and he even bunked off school to watch them live. He ended up becoming their guitar technician and toured with the band from 2006 to 2007 where he changed strings and set up equipment.

****

GQ magazine honoured Ed with the Worst Dressed Man award in 2012. "Named no.1 worst dressed male in GQ, glad they noticed. I did wear a Burberry suit once," he tweeted at the time.

Ed says he didn't release *Drunk* as a single in the USA because he felt the radio stations wouldn't play it. He was worried the song might encourage underage drinking in the country where you have to be 21 to legally consume alcohol.

****

Along with Johnny McDaid, Ed wrote the end credits song *All of the Stars* for the 2014 movie *The Fault in Our Stars*. "It was kind of inspired by the whole movie, just wanting to be sad, yet euphoric and lift people a little bit, which I hope it does," said Ed.

Ed Sheeran

At the age of 12, Ed performed what he considers to be his first 'proper' gig at a youth club in Framlingham. It was for an X Factor-type contest and Ed beat a local band to be named the overall winner!

****

A Heinz tomato ketchup bottle is one of Ed's many tattoos and the singer insists on having the sauce with his chips. Ed even made time to visit the Heinz History Center in Pittsburgh while on tour to marvel at the multitude of condiment exhibits.

Ed Sheeran

Ed has won two prestigious Ivor Novello awards – which recognises the UK and Ireland's best songwriters and composers. The first came in 2012 for the Best Song Musically and Lyrically with *The A Team*. Four years later, Ed was crowned Songwriter of the Year.

****

Ed was once given a Barbie doll for a birthday present by his older brother Matthew. He says it was the worst gift he has ever received.

The song *I See Fire* was written by Ed for *The Hobbit: The Desolation of Smaug.* It was played over the closing credits and reached No.1 in New Zealand where much of the film was shot. He was given one of the swords from the film by director Sir Peter Jackson.

****

Ed has been given the title of Baron von Edward Sheeran of Sealand by the independent state of Sealand, which is located in the sea off East Anglia.

Gingerbread Man Records was set up by Ed
in 2015, as a subsidiary of Warner Music. He
signed Jamie Lawson and then Foy Vance who
have both previously toured with Ed. Jamie
beat Ed to a 2016 Ivor Novello award in the
Best Song Musically and Lyrically category for
Wasn't Expecting That.

****

Damien Rice was the singer who inspired Ed
to embark on a career in music. He was first
captivated by the Irishman's album *O* and had
an inspirational chat with him in a Dublin pub
after watching his gig.

Ed Sheeran

In 2014, Ed was named the most powerful figure in black and urban music by BBC Radio 1Xtra – the UK's leading black music station. Ed topped their Power List which was compiled by a panel of industry experts.

****

A girl called Claire was Ed's first love and she was the subject of his early songwriting. The tracks feature on his *The Orange Room* EP, named after his bedroom wall colours where he wrote and recorded the songs.

Ed Sheeran

One Direction's song *Moments* was given to them by Ed who wrote it himself. He has been a long-term friend of Harry Styles and Ed also played most of the instruments on the track when the band recorded it. Ed has also co-written 1D songs *Little Things* and *Over Again*.

****

Ed got experience performing in public by busking on the streets of Ireland, where he used to spend family holidays. As a 13-year-old, he sang for passing shoppers in Galway, among other places.

After moving to London, Ed enrolled at the
Access To Music college, in east London to take
its Artists Development course. Here he learned
skills such as audience analysis and marketing
to help grow his career. Ed went there for two
days a week and wrote and
recorded music the rest of the time.

****

Ed keeps a number of wild animals at his
Suffolk estate, which include: otters, herons,
hedgehogs and barn owls. He had to replace
the koi fish in his pond after the otters ate them.

A special Elton John pep talk made Ed feel more relaxed during their 2013 Grammys performance. Ed said: "When I stepped on the podium, looked around and saw who was watching, I was like, 'Aww, OK!'. Then Elton lent over and said, 'This is the worst time to get your c*ck out'. And it completely shot every nerve that I had in my body and then I played."

****

Trevor, Keith, Lloyd, Nigel, Cyril, Felix and James the Second are names given to Ed's guitars.

Ed Sheeran

The walls in Ed's London house contain signatures from stars that have visited him. They include Harry Styles, Rick Rubin and Benny Blanco, along with some artwork from Damien Hirst. One wall is solely taken up by Eric Clapton's autograph.

****

Ed decided to go to university in Guildford to study music – but had barely started the course when he quit. A promoter offered him the chance to go on tour with pop star Just Jack which was an opportunity he could not turn down.

Ed Sheeran

There was no TV in the Sheeran household when Ed was a kid. His parents believed playing music or painting would be more stimulating for him and his brother. The only thing they would watch would be the occasional *Pingu* or *Blackadder* video.

****

A pig-shaped statue named 'Ed Sheer-Ham' was unveiled as part of a Pigs Gone Wild art trail in Ipswich in 2016. Ed bought it for £6,200 at a charity auction with proceeds going to the local hospice.

Some of the songs co-written by Ed for other artists include: Olly Murs' *Love Shine Down*; Rudimental's *Lay it All On Me*; Jessie Ware's *Say You Love Me*; Wretch 32's *Hush Little Baby*; Lupe Fiasco's *Old School Love*; Naughty Boy's *Top Floor (Cabana)*; Hilary Duff's *Tattoo*; Wiley's *If I Could*; The Weeknd's *Dark Times* and Taylor Swift's *Everything Has Changed*.

****

Ed went on *The Voice USA* to help Christina Aguilera mentor contestants in 2013. He returned a year later and sang *All of the Stars* with contestant Christina Grimmie in the finale.

Ed's first-ever gig in London when he moved to the capital was at a pub called The Liberties – now named the Camden Head – on Camden High Street. He also played at The World's End and T-Bird in Finsbury Park and the Cobden Club in Kensal Rise.

****

Older brother Matthew is an award-winning classical music composer who specialises in music for film and TV. They collaborated for the first time on Ed's song *Perfect* with Matthew doing the orchestration.

Ed Sheeran

Ed was raised in Framlingham in Suffolk, which was named the best place to live in Britain by Country Life magazine in 2006. It was described as the "essence of the English market town" with its history, good schools and bustling shops. Ed sings about its medieval castle in *Castle on the Hill*.

****

Ed introduced *Friends* star Courteney Cox to future fiance Johnny McDaid of Snow Patrol. Johnny popped in to visit Ed who was staying at Courtney's house in Malibu, California, and the pair hit it off straight away.

Ed Sheeran

Ed has been immortalised in wax at Madame Tussauds in the USA. "Met my waxwork at Madame Tussauds, he didn't say much but he's got a bulge so it's all good," Ed said after taking a selfie with it.

****

The video for *Shape of You* features Ed with American dancer Jennie Pegouskie and retired sumo wrestler 'Yama'. It had more than 2.5 billion views on YouTube by the end of 2017, and is the site's seventh most-watched of all time. The song also reached one billion streams on Spotify.

The video for *Drunk* – Ed's fourth single from his debut album – was the first that Ed appeared in fully. In it, a cat takes Ed out for a night of drinking to help him recover from breaking up with a girl, played by Scottish singer Nina Nesbitt who had supported Ed on tour.

****

Ed was technically homeless for most of 2008 and from 2009 to 2010. He kipped on friends' sofas, floors or even the London Tube and street! There was a warm arch outside Buckingham Palace which Ed sometimes slept under.

When on tour in Australia in 2015, Ed made an appearance as himself on popular soap *Home and Away*. Character Marilyn, who has known 'Teddy' since childhood, prepares him a meal with her friends and she doesn't realise he is a famous singer.

****

Granddad Bill used to be an amateur boxer and was involved with the British Boxing Board of Control.

Ed Sheeran

Celebrity friends Nicole Scherzinger and Taylor Swift were shown the delights of a proper English pub in Ed's home town of Framlingham. Ed took the American stars for a pint at his local boozer, The Station, on separate trips to Suffolk.

****

Ed loves grime music and has appeared as a featured artist on tracks with various UK rappers, including: Wretch 32, Devlin, Wiley and Rizzle Kicks.

Ed Sheeran

Urban music channel SB.TV played a big role in promoting the unsigned Ed by posting his videos online. Ed was the first non-rapper on its YouTube page, among the likes of up-and-coming grime acts Wretch 32 and Labrinth.

****

The huge tattoo of a lion on Ed's chest is the one that means most to him. It was inked on Ed's body as a tribute to his three sold-out shows at the England football team's stadium, Wembley.

Records were smashed when *Shape of You* went to No.1 and *Castle on the Hill* No. 2 on the UK singles chart after their double release. It was the first time in UK history an artist had achieved this. In the US, *Shape of You* became Ed's first No.1, and with *Castle on the Hill* going in at No.6, it was the first time an artist has debuted two singles in the top 10 there simultaneously.

****

Restaurant chain Nando's created a special 'Ed's Peri-Peri Sauce' with Ed's face on it.

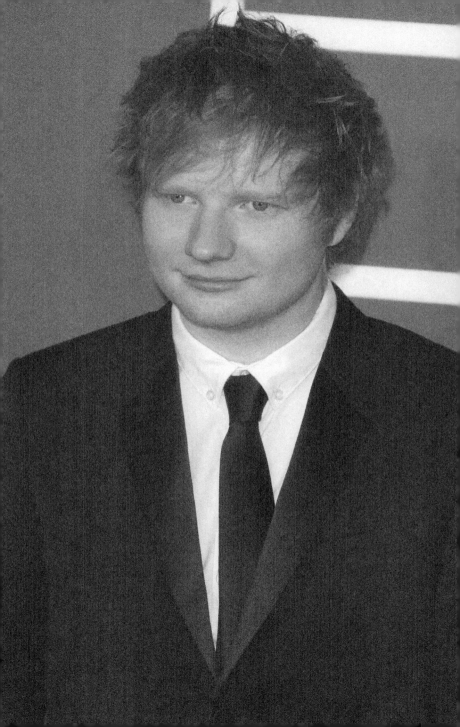

Ed's cousin Laura is an Irish singer, composer
and musician, and a dab hand at the flute,
ukulele, accordion and bowed saw. Along
with solo performances, her music has
featured in theatre productions, short films
and documentaries.

****

Talk-show queen Oprah Winfrey was interested
in offering Ed a record deal after he was making
waves in the US following his appearance on
Jamie Foxx's radio show and the buzz he made
on the Los Angeles club circuit.

Ed Sheeran

Ed produced a soulful cover of Foy Vance's song *Make It Rain* for an episode in season seven of *Sons of Anarchy*. The show's creator got in touch with Ed after he tweeted he was a fan of the show and he often performs the track on tour.

****

As a child, Ed played the cello and also the piano, attaining grade five at the age of eight. However, these days he admits: "I can't play the piano to save my life."

Ed Sheeran

He developed his singing voice while with his mum in the church choir. Ed gave up at the age of nine as he didn't want to miss out on Friday night TV, but later returned to the choir at his school.

****

As a mark of their friendship, Taylor Swift made Ed a needlepoint with mini versions of each other embroidered on it and a Drake song quote: "Started from the bottom, now we're here".

Ed donned some 14th Century garments to play the protege of a high-ranking church elder in 2015's *The Bastard Executioner*. He played Sir Cormac in five episodes of the FX historical drama but unfortunately it wasn't renewed for a second season.

****

It's hard to believe now, but Ed was often sent to detention or suspended for not doing his homework and skipping school. Not surprisingly, his favourite subject was music. "I wasn't really good at anything else if I'm honest!" admitted Ed.

The first record Ed bought was *Conspiracy of One* by *The Offspring*. He was also a fan of Linkin Park, Guns N' Roses, Blink 182 and Green Day, who Ed models his fashion sense on today!

****

Readers of Heat magazine voted Ed second in a 2014 weird crush top-ten compilation. The singer was a high climber, rising from number 10 the year before in the list of fanciable stars who are not conventionally good-looking.

Ed Sheeran

Justin Bieber's hit *Love Yourself* was co-written by Ed for ÷ but he gave it to Bieber as he says it didn't fit on his album. It became Billboard's number one song of 2016 and nominated for a Grammy. Ed also co-wrote another No.1 single in Major Lazer's *Cold Water* that features Bieber.

****

Ed's favourite bad joke is: "What do you call an elephant that doesn't mean anything? An irrelephant."

Ed Sheeran

Bruno Mars unwittingly helped get Ed picked up by a record label. At a gig in Notting Hill where the US star was performing, Ed met a talent scout from Asylum-Atlantic and the company ended up signing Ed.

****

Ed makes a point of never getting drunk before a show following an incident at a pub gig when he first moved to London. Someone pointed out that staggering around the stage was unprofessional and was not going to help get him signed.

Ed once tried his hand at acting and joined the London-based National Youth Theatre at 15. He auditioned for a new ITV musical drama series called *Britannia High* which required youngsters to be able to sing, dance and act. Ed was unsuccessful, so he decided to focus on music instead.

****

The superpower Ed says he would like to possess would be to be able to heal people. And after they've been healed, they too would have that power.

Ed was born in the West Yorkshire village of Hebden Bridge and it was once crowned the coolest place to live in Britain by The Times newspaper. It's recognised for being a quirky haven for artists, musicians, creatives and home to hippies since the 70s.

****

The song *I Will Take You Home* by Ed was premiered in a 2015 episode of *Cougar Town*. The US sitcom, which came to an end that year after six seasons, features Ed's good friend Courteney Cox.

Ed Sheeran

In 2015, Ed was awarded an honorary
doctorate from University Campus Suffolk
in Ipswich for his "outstanding contribution to
music". He spoke of his delight on social
media: "I graduated today, I am now officially
Dr Sheeran."

****

Ed was named the most-streamed artist in
the world by Spotify in 2014. With more than
860 million streams on the service, he finished
ahead of Eminem and Coldplay. Ed was No.2
on 2015's Spotify list, behind Drake.

Ed Sheeran

Radio 1 was reluctant to play Ed's first single *The A Team* as the station felt it wasn't appropriate for their audience. However, the bosses soon realised its popularity among young fans when they saw 1,000 turn up to watch Ed at a 200-capacity venue. It became the UK's bestselling debut single of the year.

****

Robinsons Fruit & Barley squash is Ed's favourite drink and he always requests it for his tour rider.

When Ed's parents eventually got a TV, his favourite shows were *Buffy the Vampire Slayer*, *Malcolm in the Middle*, *The Fresh Prince of Bel Air* and *The Simpsons*. Though mum initially disapproved of the yellow-character cartoon because she thought it was like South Park!

****

In June 2017, Ed was appointed an MBE – The Most Excellent Order of the British Empire – for services to music and charity in the Queen's Birthday Honours. The honour is a British order of chivalry and was established in 1917 by King George V.

Green Day was Ed's first live concert when he went to Wembley Arena with his dad. They travelled to many gigs together to watch the likes of Paul McCartney, Eric Clapton, Bob Dylan, Foy Vance and Damien Rice.

****

When Christmas Comes Around was co-written by Ed for *The X Factor*'s eventual winner Matt Terry in 2016. It got to number three in the UK charts and proceeds from sales went to charity.

Ed Sheeran

Thinking Out Loud was the first single to spend an entire year in the UK top 40. It was the seventh single to become triple platinum in the UK during the 21st Century, the first track to be streamed over 500 million times on Spotify and it has a staggering 1.8 billion views on YouTube. It is also the most popular 'first dance' song on Spotify.

****

After learning his first guitar chords, *A Million Miles Away* by Rory Gallagher was the first song Ed learned to play fully.

Ed Sheeran

Before Ed was signed by Asylum-Atlantic
Records, he was actually given a contract
to release a single on Island Records after
winning a music contest the company held.
The track was called *Let it Out* but afterwards
the label decided to release him. A decision
they must regret today!

****

Taylor Swift's mum Andrea Finlay once gave
Ed a wooden gramophone speaker for his
iPhone as a present. It was a consolation gift
to make up for Ed missing out on a Grammy
award in 2013.

In June 2017, Forbes magazine ranked Ed at number 71 in the World's Highest-Paid Celebrities list with earnings of $37m in a 12-month scoring period. Rapper P Diddy was number one with $130m coming into his bank account and Adele was 18th with $69m earned.

****

The majority of songs on Ed's debut album + were about Ed's ex-girlfriend Alice. The record only cost £10,000 to produce, as much of it had already been written and recorded.

Uncle Bill played a key role in Ed's musical education while he was growing up. Bill introduced Bob Dylan, Jimi Hendrix and Van Morrison to Ed's dad – and in turn – Ed himself. Bill also gave Ed his first lessons in playing the guitar.

****

One of Ed's tattoos on his arm is of a mother and child by French artist Henri Matisse. Ed bought the painting for his mum from one of his first pay cheques and it's a tribute to her.

Ed Sheeran

Ed met his current manager Stuart Camp while he was still unsigned and touring with Just Jack. Stuart was part of Elton John's Rocket Music Management and Ed spent a lot of time sleeping on his sofa!

****

Ed appeared as himself on New Zealand soap *Shortland Street* in 2014, while in the country to promote his album x. Ed gives the character Kane a pep talk before his friends turn up for lunch at a restaurant.

Ed Sheeran

A 17-year-old Ed entered an eastern England-based talent contest called the 2008 Next Big Thing. Despite breaking four guitar strings and suffering problems with his mic, Ed was a winner, and he secured a cash prize, music equipment and studio time.

****

In the 2016 film *Bridget Jones's Baby*, Ed meets Bridget at a music festival bar and she doesn't know who he is, but later twigs when Ed later appears with his guitar on stage.

A portrait of Ed Sheeran by Colin Davidson went on display at London's National Portrait Gallery in 2017. Davidson has previously painted a number of high-profile figures, including Brad Pitt, Kenneth Branagh and the Queen.

****

With a surprisingly large amount of money from digital sales of his independent EPs, a generous Ed paid off his parents' mortgage when he signed for Asylum-Atlantic Records.

Ed got builders to convert a derelict barn in his garden into a pub that's linked to his house by a tunnel. The boozer has strict operating hours and is only open to Ed's friends when he comes back home to visit them.

****

Kiss Me on the + album was a song specifically written for the wedding of Ed's godfather and godmother and the singer performed it on their big day too.

Ed Sheeran

Despite looking dishevelled with his messy hair and often appearing unshaven, Ed is a clean freak. He says he showers twice a day and has a bottle of hand sanitiser with him at all times. Paco Rabanne Million is his aftershave of choice.

****

Irish singer Gary Dunne was the inspiration for Ed to learn effects on a loop pedal after watching him open for Nizlopi at the Shepherd's Bush Empire in 2005.

Ed Sheeran

Ed's cat Graham was active on Twitter for a while in 2014. The singer set up the account for his feline friend and @GrahamShizza tweeted 58 times and attracted 69,000 followers.

****

To celebrate Ed's 26th birthday, Pizza Express created a pizza cake called the 'Ed-Abrese', which was made from the ingredients featured on his favourite pizza, the Calabrese.

An unsigned Ed once played a gig to an empty venue in Exeter with just a promoter and a sound engineer watching. He was paid £50, but the train ticket to the West Country cost him £80. Ouch.

****

In 2014, Ed performed two concerts for British troops at Camp Bastion in Afghanistan, organised by The British Forces Foundation. Ed chatted with soldiers and visited the towers around the perimeter during his visit.

Ed fit 55 Maltesers in his mouth while appearing on James Corden's *Carpool Karaoke*, beating his previous record of 40 set when he was a teenager in a YouTube video.

****

Ed joined the 2014 incarnation of charity supergroup Band Aid 30 to record a version of *Do They Know It's Christmas?* to raise money for the Ebola virus epidemic in West Africa. He lent his vocals with Ellie Goulding, One Direction, Emeli Sande, Sam Smith, Rita Ora and Bastille on the track.

Ed Sheeran

The singer's third album ÷ has broken multiple UK records. It became the fastest-selling by a male solo artist in British chart history; the third fastest-seller ever (behind Adele and Oasis); it got the biggest one-week vinyl sales in more than two decades and all 16 tracks appeared in the top 20 due to its high streaming figures.

****

Ed's childhood friend Phillip Butah produced the artwork for his albums and also an illustrated book of his life. Ed's art consultant parents have worked with Phillip since he was 15.

Ed Sheeran

Ed's mum Imogen creates her own jewellery and her designs include Liquorice Allsorts bracelets for Ed. The Duchess of Cambridge, Kate Middleton, along with Jessie J and Rupert Grint have all worn the homemade pieces.

****

US rapper Yelawolf recorded a four-track EP *The Slumdon Bridge* with Ed in 2012. Ed said: "We hooked up for 10 hours in the studio and made four songs from scratch. He's into rock 'n' roll and punk music. I'm into folk music and shades of singer-songwriter stuff. We put all our influences in a big bowl and mixed them."

When Ed was an unsigned act, he even performed at people's houses to make ends meet. Charging £100, he would also get food and a bed for the night as part of the package.

****

Lego was the inspiration behind *Lego House* but it's also what makes Ed relax when he's not performing. He said: "When you make Lego, you're so engrossed with the instructions and finding the little bits and putting it all together, you don't think of anything else. And you're doing it for six or seven hours, so you switch off and make it."

One reason for having + as Ed's debut album title in 2011 was to stop people from finding it to illegally download. "You can't Google it so it's quite hard to find on torrenting sites," he said. "I have to make a living and musicians don't make much money these days. I've never illegally downloaded anything, I've always bought CDs."

****

One of the favourite karaoke songs that Ed performs is 90s R&B song *Pony* by US singer Ginuwine.

Ed Sheeran

Ed had stammer as a young boy but says he was able to cure it after constantly reciting the fast-paced rap lyrics from Eminem's *The Marshall Mathers LP*.

****

Ed has embraced social media since his days as an unsigned act and is one of the most popular musicians online. After the release of his album ÷ in 2017, he had 15.6 million Instagram followers, 20.4 million on Twitter, 17 million on Facebook and 21.7 million are subscribed to his YouTube channel.

Ed Sheeran

London-born Emil Nava is the director behind many of Ed's music videos. Ed got him on board for *You Need Me* in 2011 and he's gone on to produce many more, including: *Lego House*, *Thinking Out Loud*, *Bloodstream* and *Sing*, which won Best Male Video at the 2014 MTV Video Music Awards.

****

Ed's grandparents hail from County Wexford in Ireland and *Nancy Mulligan* is based on his grandmother. He has cousins all over the Emerald Isle, from Dublin to Cork and Galway, and Ed visits as often as he can.

The video for *You Need Me* has actor Matthew Morgan perform the lyrics in British Sign Language. "We found a concept that hadn't been done which was sign language to highlight the lyrical aspect to it," said Ed.

****

James Bond fan Ed once bought himself an Aston Martin, one of the sports cars driven by the fictional English spy. However, Ed said he felt like such an idiot driving it through his home town that he lent it to his manager's wife for six months.

Martin is the guitar of choice for Ed, ever since he used its travel-friendly Backpacker version during his couch-surfing days. Martin created a custom-made 'Divide' signature guitar to celebrate Ed's album, with the singer donating the sales to East Anglia's Children's Hospices.

****

Ed appeared on TIME magazine's The 100 Most Influential People list of 2017. His entry was written by Taylor Swift, who said: "Congratulations to my friend Ed, for the legacy you've already built and the brilliant hook you probably just came up with five minutes ago."

Ed Sheeran

Radio, which is a song about not getting on the airwaves, was Ed's first to get played. He heard it on Radio 1 while in his then-girlfriend's car when she was driving, but they only managed to hear 10 seconds of it after the station had cut out.

****

Some of the biggest magazine front covers Ed has appeared on include: Vanity Fair, NME, Q Magazine, OK!, Rolling Stone, Billboard and British GQ.

Ed Sheeran

Ed's childhood ambition was to drive a train for a living and he still hasn't given up hope. "I remember being four and wanting to be a train driver – that was the only thing that interested me. I'll become a train driver one day," he said.

****

Ed believes in the Malcolm Gladwell theory that it takes 10,000 hours of doing anything to master it. He said in 2015: "I read that when I was 13, because John Mayer used to talk about it. I think it's true. I'm coming up to 10,000 hours, and I'm now a professional musician. So it definitely does work."

Ed picked the 'Sheerios' name himself to describe his loyal band of fans. He said: "They were calling themselves the Sheeranators and it felt really awkward on TV interviews. I was brainstorming and I thought [Sheerios] sounded funny. I didn't name them, I literally just said I approve and nothing else. But I do find it a bit weird, a fan base having a name."

****

After being inspired by James Morrison, who performed 200 gigs in a single year and got signed, Ed reached an incredible total of 300 throughout 2009 (reportedly 312, in fact).

Ed Sheeran

Ed was born on February 17, 1991, and he shares his birthday with a number of famous faces. They include: socialite Paris Hilton, basketball legend Michael Jordan, actor Joseph Gordon-Levitt and former British Olympic swimmer Rebecca Adlington.

****

In a nod to his Celtic roots, Ed made a special Irish language version of *Thinking Out Loud* in 2015. Translated as *Ag Smaoineamh Os Ard*, Ed learned the song's words in Gaelic and recorded it while on tour in Australia for a compilation CD sent to Irish school children.

Ed was teased at school for looking like fellow ginger Ron Weasley from the Harry Potter films. And it's why he chose the character's actor Rupert Grint to play himself in the video for *Lego House*. With Ed being a big fan of Harry Potter, it made it extra special.

****

Give Me Love has featured in four TV shows – supernatural drama *The Vampire Diaries*, Aussie soap *Home and Away*, US sitcom *Cougar Town* and lawyer drama *Reckless*.

Printed in Great Britain
by Amazon